CHIEF JOSEPH
GUARDIAN OF HIS PEOPLE

BY ELIZABETH RIDER MONTGOMERY

ILLUSTRATED BY FRANK VAUGHN

GARRARD PUBLISHING COMPANY
CHAMPAIGN, ILLINOIS

ALICE MARRIOTT and CAROL K. RACHLIN of Southwest Research Associates are consultants for Garrard Indian Books. They are presently joint artists-in-residence in the Division of Language Arts at Central State College, Edmond, Oklahoma.

MISS MARRIOTT has lived among the Kiowa and Cheyenne Indians in Oklahoma and spent many years with the Pueblos of New Mexico and the Hopis of Arizona. First woman to take a degree in anthropology from the University of Oklahoma, she is a Fellow of the American Anthropological Association, now working with its Curriculum Project.

MISS RACHLIN, also a Fellow of AAA and of the American Association for the Advancement of Science, is a graduate in anthropology of Columbia University. She has done archaeological work in New Jersey and Indiana, and ethnological field work with Algonquian tribes of the Midwest.

Contents

The Nez Perces

Joseph's people, the Nez Perces (pronounced "Nez Purses"), lived in the basin area of the Snake and Columbia Rivers in what is today Idaho, Oregon, and Washington. The Nez Perce tribe was divided into bands on a village or geographical basis. Each village had its own chief, fishing place, and strip of territory along the river.

The Nez Perces had several kinds of houses, including a tepee structure and underground lodges. The most important kind of house was a long dwelling shaped like an A-tent, which housed many families.

Since the Nez Perces did not grow their own crops, they depended mainly on wild foods. Game such as elk, deer, and mountain sheep were fairly plentiful, as was salmon at certain times of the year. Their most important food was the camas plant, which they ate either raw or cooked. Their clothing was made primarily from elk, buffalo, or deer hides, which they decorated with beads, porcupine quills, and paint.

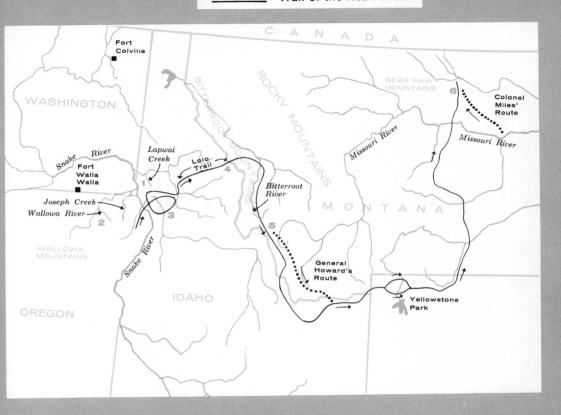

1. Lapwai, where young Joseph and his brother attended the Presbyterian mission school.

2. Wallowa, the summer home of Joseph's people, near the mountains where Joseph kept his sacred vigil.

3. White Bird Canyon, where soldiers fired on Joseph's truce flag and the battle began.

4. Where Captain Rawn attempted to keep the Nez Perces from entering Montana.

5. Big Hole Basin, where General Gibbon's soldiers fired into the sleeping Nez Perce camp, killing and wounding many Indians.

6. Bear Paw Mountains, where Colonel Miles' army surrounded the Nez Perces and Joseph surrendered.

1

No More Mission School

Seven-year-old Joseph showed his neat printing to his little brother.

"See this, Ollokot," he said proudly. "These are Nez Perce words. I will show you how to print them."

In the little schoolroom, the two small Indian boys bent over their papers. As they worked, they read aloud in Nez Perce, "Our Father, Who Art in Heaven . . ." All around them other Indians said their lessons aloud, too.

It was the year 1847, in what is now western Idaho. Joseph and Ollokot were the sons of Tu-eka-kas, a wealthy Nez Perce chief. The boys attended the Presbyterian mission school at Lapwai run by Mr. and Mrs. Spalding. These missionaries were teaching Nez Perces to read and write. They wanted the Indians to become Christians. They also wanted them to be farmers so they would settle down in one place.

Mrs. Spalding came to look at Joseph's work. "That is fine, Joseph," she said. "Ollokot is doing well, too. Soon you can both read your father's Bible."

Joseph had often seen his father's "Bible," the Gospel of Matthew printed in Nez Perce. The chief was very proud of it.

8

Now Mrs. Spalding smiled down at earnest Joseph and laughing Ollokot.

"Your father is a true Christian," she told them. "He is a fine man and a good chief."

The schoolroom door opened. Chief Tu-eka-kas, tall and proud, stalked in.

"Come, my sons," the chief roared. "We are returning to Wallowa."

"Oh, no!" protested Mrs. Spalding. "Do not take the boys out of school."

"A white man put shame on me," the chief announced. "He gave me a worn-out blanket." A government man, who was passing out blankets to Indians, had given Chief Tu-eka-kas a blanket with holes.

"I am not a poor man," Tu-eka-kas stormed. "I need no such gift."

9

In spite of everything Mrs. Spalding said, the chief took Joseph and Ollokot out of school.

The people of Tu-eka-kas' band had set up their village near the mission buildings. Now they all began to pack. Joseph's sisters helped their mother,

10

Arenoth, take down the tepees and roll the buffalo-skin coverings. They helped her tie the lodge poles into bundles. They packed the family's blankets, the tightly coiled baskets used for cooking, their wooden eating bowls, and their horn spoons.

Joseph and Ollokot gathered up the fishing gear, while their older brother, Sousouquee, helped men round up horses and cattle. Then the Wallowa band of Nez Perces left the Lapwai mission. Joseph rode up front by his father and his brothers. His school days were over. His father would never forgive the white people for insulting him.

2

Boyhood in Wallowa

In Wallowa Valley Joseph soon forgot most of what he had learned in school. His days were busy and happy.

Wallowa, in eastern Oregon, was the beloved summer home of Tu-eka-kas' people. All other Nez Perce bands acknowledged that the valley belonged to them. High mountains guarded the valley. The lake and rivers were full of fish. Every morning when the sun peeped over the mountains, the village crier rode among the lodges shouting:

"I wonder if everyone is up! It is morning. Rise up! Go see to the horses, lest a wolf has killed one. Thanks be that we are alive!"

Arenoth came from the tepee to stir the fire. Joseph and Ollokot came out too. They bathed in the river.

After breakfast the boys got on their horses. The Nez Perces raised very fine horses. Even the smallest children were good horsemen. With other Nez Perce boys, Joseph raced along the lake shore. He was learning to hang on one side of his horse while shooting an arrow from under the horse's neck.

When they tired of racing, Joseph and his brother came back to the village. They watched Arenoth cook camas roots in pits lined with stones and roast

salmon and venison over open fires. They saw their sisters scraping deer hides, which would be used to make clothing.

The little boys watched their father's skillful work on a new bow made from a mountain sheep's horn. They watched Sousouquee and other young warriors decorate war bonnets with eagle feathers.

"Someday I shall wear a war bonnet," Ollokot said. "I will be a brave warrior."

"I shall be a chief," said Joseph. "I shall take care of my people."

In the evenings the Indians gathered around fires in the longhouse. This was a big building 150 feet long. The roof was covered with cattail mats. Down the center was a row of fires.

Joseph enjoyed these evenings. Old men repeated stories and myths, teaching the children tribal history and legend.

One man told about the coming of the Lewis and Clark expedition to Nez Perce country. The Nez Perces promised to keep peace with the white people forever.

"Our people have never broken that promise," Tu-eka-kas told his sons.

A storyteller told about the coming of the missionaries. Another explained how some French trappers named the tribe "Nez Perce," or "Pierced Nose," because some men wore nose ornaments.

Although they had heard these stories over and over again, Joseph and Ollokot always listened eagerly.

Other Indians told the young children all about their tribe. "Our Nez Perce nation has a number of bands," they said.

"Each band has its own village, its own fishing and hunting grounds, and its own chief. Village council meetings are held with chief and headmen. Tribal councils are held with the chiefs of different bands. In any Nez Perce council, all must agree, or there is no decision. A chief can speak only for his own band."

Sometimes men spoke of the greatness of the Nez Perce nation. "We are the biggest, the richest, and the strongest Indian tribe in this land," they said proudly. "Our beautiful Appaloosa horses are famous. We raise excellent cattle, too, and we have miles and miles of grazing land."

Joseph's eyes shone as he listened. How proud he was to be a Nez Perce!

3

The Sacred Vigil

The happy seasons passed. Joseph's father taught him to hunt, to fish, and to make spears, knives, and arrows. He taught him to imitate the calls of birds and animals.

Joseph learned the Indian Spirit Laws too. He learned that the Great Spirit sees and hears everything. Joseph understood that he must treat others the way he wanted to be treated. He learned that lying is the very worst sin, especially if the lie is told three times.

When Joseph was about thirteen, Chief Tu-eka-kas said to him, "It is time to keep your sacred vigil, my son."

Very early the next morning, Joseph prepared for his vigil. Naked, unarmed, he left the village and the valley. Up, up into the mountains he climbed. At last he reached the top of a ridge, where he built a little heap of stones.

Far below him, Joseph could see Lake Wallowa and the big valley. The village on the lake shore looked very tiny. The boy closed his eyes and began to pray. He prayed to the Christian God and to the Indians' Great Spirit. Sometimes he thought that they were the same God.

For hours Joseph prayed and waited but no guardian spirit came. When night fell he made a little fire to keep

from freezing. He could hear animals moving nearby but he was not afraid. Nothing would hurt a young Indian keeping the sacred vigil. His eyes grew heavy but he would not sleep.

The night dragged on. Daylight came. Joseph was hungry but he would not think about food. He was very thirsty but he would not think about water. He kept on praying.

As the day passed, Joseph began to feel light-headed. That night a storm came up. Wind blew, rain fell, lightning flashed, and thunder rolled.

Finally Joseph could not keep his eyes open. In spite of the noise of the storm, he lay on the ground and slept. While he was sleeping, Joseph had a vivid dream.

On a loud roll of thunder, a man seemed to float in the air. A blanket trailed behind him. With each crash of thunder, the blanket leaped and waved.

"My boy," said the dream figure, "look at me. I am Thunder. I will give you my power, if you always do what I tell you."

The dream figure, Thunder, then taught Joseph a song and a dance that would be his alone throughout his life.

When Joseph woke he said joyfully, "Thunder is my guardian spirit." He knew that this was a very fine omen, or sign, for the things that live in the sky are powerful guardian spirits.

Joseph returned to his village. "The Great Spirit was good to me," he told his father. Joseph bathed and then his mother brought him food. He lay down on a grass bed in the tepee and slept.

Several moons later the Guardian Spirit Dance was held for those who had kept the sacred vigil. Joseph dressed carefully for it. His deerskin shirt and leggings had been cleaned with white clay from the lake shore. He put on his finest moccasins and hung many strings of beads around his neck. He wove narrow strips of fur into his long braids. He painted his face with red and yellow paint. Then he threw his richest blanket around his shoulders.

The Dance of the Guardian Spirit was held in the longhouse. Soon it was Joseph's turn to perform. He stepped into the light of the flickering fires. Joseph sang his special song and shuffled

his feet in his dance. He made motions with his hands, his arms, his entire body. His blanket leaped and waved to show that Thunder was his guardian spirit.

Other Indians began to sing with Joseph. By the time he finished his dance, everybody was singing with him.

"Him-mut-too-yah-lat-kekt," they sang. "Joseph's name is now Thunder-Rolling-in-the-Mountains."

"It is a good name," the old men said approvingly.

Joseph and Ollokot exchanged happy smiles.

4

The Great Council

Tu-eka-kas knew that his sons should learn about the responsibilities of a Nez Perce chief. He often called them from their games. They listened as he decided disputes among families. They saw how he kept thoughtless young men under control. They learned that a chief had no power to force his people to obey. He ruled by convincing them that his advice was wise and his decisions just.

Many white men were coming to the Indians' land now. They came over a road called the Oregon Trail. Nez Perce men sometimes went to meet them and trade horses for cattle.

A few white people came to Wallowa Valley and built homes and made farms. At first the Indians did not object.

"There is plenty of room here for all," Tu-eka-kas told his people.

Soon, however, many of the white settlers seemed to think that they owned Wallowa Valley. They took more and more land. Quarrels arose between the white men and the Indians.

When Joseph was fifteen, Governor Stevens, the new white governor in the Northwest, invited all Indian tribes to a council in the Walla Walla Valley.

Sousouquee, Joseph, and Ollokot went to the council with Tu-eka-kas. Of the 5,000 Indians who attended, half were Nez Perces. They set up their tepees by the river.

The council met near the governor's tent. The governor sat on a bench, while the Indians gathered around him on the ground. Tu-eka-kas and other chiefs sat in front with their sub-chiefs behind them. Joseph and Ollokot stood in the background.

"I will open my heart to you," Governor Stevens said. "I speak for our President in Washington. He sends you greetings. He loves the Indians as if they were his own children. He wants to help you."

Joseph wondered what the President

could do for the Nez Perces that they could not do for themselves.

"Many white men have come west to build houses and make farms. If Indians and white people are to live in peace, the Indians must have 'reservations, or land set aside for them."

Those words puzzled Joseph. Wouldn't it be simpler and fairer to keep white men out of Indian country?

Governor Stevens explained his plan. The Nez Perce reservation would include Wallowa Valley and Lapwai, and the Indians would be paid for the land they gave up. Schools and sawmills would be built. Indians would be given tools, clothes, and money.

Many Indian chiefs objected.

"The Earth Mother is for all men,"

Chief Tu-eka-kas argued. "No man owns her. No man can buy her. None can sell her."

Joseph nodded. His father spoke the truth. But Governor Stevens did not listen to the wise words of Chief Tu-eka-kas.

The council continued for many days. Each day the Indians listened to the governor. Each evening they spent in their villages. Joseph and Ollokot joined in the horse races and games with other Nez Perce boys. Ollokot won many of the races and Joseph was proud of his brother.

One evening Joseph went to the council fire where all the men were discussing the governor's plan. Some of the young men wanted to fight to keep their homeland. Older men counseled peace.

"Indians can never win a war against white armies," Tu-eka-kas said. "In all the seasons the white man has been pushing westward, Indians have never won a war."

So on June 11, 1855, Tu-eka-kas put his mark on Governor Stevens' treaty.

When they returned to Wallowa, Tu-eka-kas said, "We will plant poles around our valley." Joseph and Ollokot helped mark part of the Nez Perce reservation with tall poles.

"Now," said their father, "white people will know this is Nez Perce land."

"My father is very wise," thought Joseph. "We will have no more trouble with white people."

5

"The Thief Treaty"

However, the poles did not keep white people out of Wallowa Valley. Gold was found in nearby mountains, and miners poured into the valley. Troubles between red men and white became worse.

Joseph and Ollokot grew to be tall, handsome young men. Ollokot, gay and fun-loving, was a fine athlete and an expert hunter. Sometimes he would go hunting for buffalo east of the Rocky Mountains. Joseph was more serious and thoughtful. Although he was a good hunter and a strong athlete, he did not often participate in sports. He spent much time with his father and learned to think like him.

The white man's law puzzled Joseph. If an Indian killed a settler or stole from him, the Indian was punished. But a white man could steal from an Indian or kill him, and nothing was done. There seemed to be one law for Indians and another for white men.

Joseph was bothered because the United States Government did not keep the promises Governor Stevens had made.

No school was built on the Nez Perce reservation and no money came for the Indians. It was said this was because the United States Senate had not ratified the treaty. Joseph could not understand this. White people seemed to have too many chiefs.

After four years the Senate finally ratified the treaty, and the government sent money to the tribes. But Tu-eka-kas would not take any.

"Never accept any presents from the government," the old chief told Joseph. "If you do, someday they will say you sold your land."

One sad day Joseph's older brother, Sousouquee, was accidentally killed. Tu-eka-kas grieved deeply for his oldest son, and Joseph's heart ached for him.

In 1863, the government called another Nez Perce council to make a new treaty. Joseph, now twenty-three, and Ollokot took their feeble, ailing father to Lapwai. The council was conducted by Indian commissioners sent by the government.

"We cannot spare so much land for your tribe," they told the Nez Perces. "You must give up 10,000 square miles. The Lapwai area must do for all Nez Perces."

Joseph was stunned. All of Wallowa would be taken from his people!

"No!" cried Tu-eka-kas. "We will not give up the land of our fathers."

"No!" shouted Chief Looking Glass and Chief White Bird.

"No!" cried Chief Too-hool-hool-zote and Chief Hush-hush-cute.

One of the commissioners turned to Chief Lawyer. "What do *you* say to this new treaty?" he asked.

Lawyer's land would not be affected by the new treaty.

"Yes," said Lawyer. "I accept the new treaty."

The commissioner said, "Lawyer speaks for all Nez Perces."

Joseph rose. "Wallowa has been the homeland of my people for centuries," he said. "Lawyer cannot sell what is not his."

Still the commissioners did not listen. They had Lawyer and some of his sub-chiefs make their marks on the treaty. "You must move to Lapwai," Tu-eka-kas was told. "You do not own Wallowa Valley now."

"If we ever owned the land, we own it still," Joseph insisted.

"Lawyer sold the land," they answered.

"Suppose," said Joseph, "a white man comes to me and says, 'Joseph, I want to buy your horses.' I say, 'No, I will not sell them.'

"Then the white man goes to my neighbor and says, 'I want to buy Joseph's horses, but he will not sell.' My neighbor offers, 'Pay me the money and I will sell you Joseph's horses.'

"The white man returns to me and says, 'Your neighbor sold me your horses.' Do you think I would give them up?"

The commissioners repeated, "Wallowa no longer belongs to you."

Old Tu-eka-kas shouted, "I tear up your thief treaty!" He tore the paper

to bits. Then he took his precious Bible out of the folds of his blanket. With a mighty effort he tore it too.

"I tear up the white man's religion!" the old chief cried. "From where the sun now stands, I will have nothing that belongs to the white man!"

Tu-eka-kas stalked out of the council. Joseph, Ollokot, and all their people followed.

6

Chief Joseph

The Nez Perces were now like two separate tribes. Chief Lawyer's band and several others were called treaty Indians, because they had signed the "thief treaty." The rest were called nontreaty Indians and they were considered to be troublemakers because they had refused to sign.

Joseph shared his father's fury and grief over the "thief treaty." But in his

own life he had found great happiness. He had fallen in love.

The girl, called Springtime, was a member of Lawyer's band. Joseph had met her during the Lapwai council. Every evening he had played sweet music on his wooden flute outside her tepee. Soon he knew that Springtime loved him too.

Then Joseph went to Springtime's father and asked permission to marry her. Her father agreed.

When the wedding day came, Joseph's mother and sisters went to Springtime's village and brought her to Wallowa. She wore a gay pointed hat and a dress of deerskin with beautiful beading and fringe. Joseph thought she was the loveliest girl he had ever seen.

Now Joseph and Springtime had a tepee of their own. Soon they had a little daughter, Sound-of-Running-Feet. About this time Ollokot married too. The brothers' lodges were close together, and the two families were devoted to each other.

Every day Joseph went to see his aged father. Tu-eka-kas was nearly blind now. When he rode his horse, a small boy sat in front of him. Day by day he became weaker. Now Joseph acted as chief in his father's place.

One day Tu-eka-kas sent for Joseph. When he entered the tepee, Joseph knew his father was dying.

"My son," said the old chief, "my body is going to see the Great Spirit."

Joseph bowed his head.

"When I am gone," the dying man went on, "think of your country. Never sell this land."

Joseph pressed his father's hand. "I will never sell it," Joseph promised. Chief Tu-eka-kas died peacefully. He was buried in beautiful Wallowa Valley.

Then the head men of the village met in council and elected Joseph as their chief. He was thirty-one years old.

Ollokot was glad and proud. "You will be a great chief, my brother," he said. "Always I will help you."

Trouble with white men increased. Settlers tried to keep Nez Perces off their land. They stole Appaloosa horses and Nez Perce cattle. They accused Indians of stealing livestock. Indians who protested were killed. With great difficulty Joseph kept his young men from fighting back.

Time after time Joseph rode up to Lapwai and complained to the Indian agent, but nothing was done.

Sometimes the young braves accused Joseph of being a coward, but wise men knew it took more courage to endure insults than to fight back.

One autumn Joseph and his people went to Camas Meadows to gather their winter supply of camas roots. The young men rode ahead. Soon they returned, very angry.

"White settlers have ruined our camas crop!" they cried. "Their pigs have dug up the roots."

"Because the roots grow wild," said Joseph, "the white men think they are

unimportant. Come, my people. We will find another camas field." He turned his horse around. The young braves grumbled, but they followed him.

Joseph tried to make the new settlers understand what the Indians thought. He tried without success to persuade them all to leave Wallowa. For years Joseph and his people suffered many, many wrongs.

Finally, Joseph rode to Lapwai again to see John Monteith, who was the new Indian agent.

"For many winters," Joseph said, "I have been talking to the white people. It is strange that they do not yet understand what I say. Let me go to Washington and talk to the President."

Mr. Monteith refused. However, he

wrote to the President, and the President issued an order: "Wallowa Valley is not to be settled by white men. It is reserved for Nez Perce Indians."

Joseph was happy.

But white men protested that a valley the size of Massachusetts was too much to give to Indians. So the President changed his mind and opened Wallowa to settlers.

"The President speaks with a forked tongue," said Joseph bitterly.

7

Thirty Days to Move

Every year Mr. Monteith visited Chief Joseph. He brought presents and money. Each time he said, "You must move to the Lapwai Reservation."

Joseph was always courteous, but he accepted no presents or money. "We want nothing from the government," he said. "My people are satisfied here in Wallowa."

At last the government sent one-armed General Howard to Lapwai with an army. He had lost an arm in the Civil War. The general invited Joseph to a council. The other nontreaty Nez Perce chiefs went too.

"The United States Government orders you to move to the reservation," said the general.

Too-hool-hool-zote spoke hotly. "The Great Spirit made part of the world for us to live on. Where do you get the authority to say we should not live there?"

"I am the white war chief of this country," General Howard answered sharply. "Do you deny my authority? I will put you in jail!" And he did.

The young braves wanted revenge.

"No," said Joseph. "The arrest is wrong, but we must not break the peace."

The council went on for several days. Finally General Howard snapped, "Talk is useless. I must carry out my orders."

Joseph looked at Ollokot and the other chiefs. They all knew that they must move to the reservation or fight the United States Army.

"My people are like deer," Joseph said to the one-armed general. "Your people are like grizzly bears. We cannot hold our own against you. We will move to the reservation."

"You are wise, Joseph," said General Howard. "I will expect you here in thirty days with all your people."

"Why are you in such a hurry?"

asked Joseph. "Thirty suns is not half enough time." He explained that their horses and cattle were scattered. The rivers were high with spring floods and would be dangerous to cross.

General Howard repeated stubbornly: "Thirty days is all you can have. My soldiers will come if you are late. Then you will lose all your horses and cattle."

Finally Joseph agreed.

When he reached Wallowa, Joseph's daughter, Sound-of-Running-Feet, ran excitedly to meet him.

"Soldiers are here!" she cried.

Joseph was angry. General Howard had not waited thirty days!

Joseph called a council. As he had expected, the young men wanted to fight. Older men were undecided.

Joseph advised against fighting. "Let us go to the reservation at once."

Sadly the people packed to leave their homeland. Men went to round up horses and cattle. Many animals had ranged too far to be rounded up and had to be left behind.

Out of Wallowa Valley rode the Nez Perce band—500 men, women, old people, and children. Packed on horses were all their belongings. The people were sad. Joseph's heart was heavy, too.

The Snake River was dangerously high. Women, children, and family treasures were placed on rafts. With a mounted warrior at each corner, the rafts were ferried across the river.

Then the men drove the livestock into the stream. Suddenly a fierce rainstorm

came up, and many animals were swept far down the river. While the Indians worked to save them, white men came and stole many Appaloosa horses.

At last the Indians reached Rocky Canyon, just outside the boundary line of the reservation. The other nontreaty bands were assembled there. A grand council was held, and there was much war talk. Joseph had great difficulty in getting the council to agree to peace.

When he thought the danger of war was over, Joseph went to butcher some beef for his family. As he was returning, he heard dreadful news. White Bird's young braves had killed four white men.

Sadly Joseph followed as the other Indians rode to White Bird Canyon. War was unavoidable now.

8

War!

At dawn soldiers came riding down into White Bird Canyon. Joseph sent six warriors with a white truce flag to meet them. But soldiers fired on the flag of truce, and the battle began.

There were only 60 Indian fighters, and few had guns, but it seemed as if there were hundreds. Their heads bobbed up from rocks or brush to fire, then they dropped out of sight. A herd of horses galloped through the army's lines, with Indians hanging from the horses' sides and shooting from under their necks. The soldiers retreated.

Because Joseph had been the spokesman for the nontreaty Indians for years, General Howard held him responsible for the fighting. He sent word that if Joseph surrendered, the other Indians could go free. But Joseph knew that the white men had never kept their word to the Indians, so he would not surrender.

The Indians elected Looking Glass as war chief. Joseph was chosen guardian of the families, because all the people trusted him. And the Nez Perces started east across the Bitterroot Mountains on the Lolo Trail, a steep, dangerous trail 250 miles long.

When they had almost finished their terrible eleven-day journey across Idaho, scouts brought bad news.

"A fort has been built across Lolo Trail," the scouts said. "Captain Rawn's soldiers threaten to keep us out of Montana."

The chiefs went to the fort to talk to Captain Rawn.

"We wish to go through this country," said Looking Glass.

"We come in peace," said Joseph.

"You may pass," Captain Rawn answered, "if you give me your guns, ammunition, and horses."

"No," replied Joseph. "Without horses, our families cannot travel. Without guns, we would be at the mercy of any soldiers we met."

"Then you cannot pass," replied the captain.

The chiefs returned to their people.

Joseph sent young men to find a way out of the canyon, and they cleared another trail. It was hidden from the fort and out of rifle range.

The next morning a few warriors began to fire on the fort. While the soldiers were busy firing back, Joseph took the families and baggage over the new trail.

Now that they were in Montana, the Nez Perces thought they were safe.

"We left the war and General Howard in Idaho," said Joseph.

On August 7, the Indians camped in Big Hole Basin. Looking Glass, their war chief, would not post sentries.

Under Joseph's direction, the people cut lodge poles, caught fish, and shot game. For two days everybody worked.

Before dawn the third day, General Gibbon, who was in charge of that area, found the sleeping camp. Soldiers fired into tepees, killing women, children, and warriors. Springtime, Joseph's wife, and Fair Land, Ollokot's wife, were wounded. Fair Land died soon after.

When the soldiers retreated to the bluffs above the camp, Joseph gathered the women, children, old people, and the injured. He led them away, while warriors fought off the soldiers.

On went the fleeing Indians, and the soldiers followed them. General Howard caught up with General Gibbon, and they both pursued Chief Joseph.

One day Looking Glass protested, "Why do we hurry? Our people are tired, and our horses lame."

"We must reach Canada," Joseph said.

"The one-armed general is four suns behind us," said Looking Glass. "We do not have to travel so fast."

The other chiefs agreed, and Joseph said no more.

On September 29 the Indians camped at the foot of Bear Paw Mountains only a few miles from Canada and freedom. The next morning a new army under Colonel Miles found them!

Joseph was with the horse herd, away from the lodges, helping families pack their belongings. Suddenly he saw some soldiers riding down the hill.

"Hurry!" he shouted to his daughter, helping her onto a horse. "Ride north! Find Sitting Bull in Canada. Ask him to send warriors!"

Sound-of-Running-Feet rode quickly away as did all women and children who were ready. But many could not leave, for soldiers surrounded the camp.

Joseph was cut off from the camp. Unarmed, he dashed through their lines. His horse was wounded, and his clothes were bullet-riddled.

His wife met him at the door of their lodge. "Here is your gun!" she cried. "Fight!"

The Indians soon drove the soldiers back up the hill. But many brave Nez Perces had been killed, including Ollokot and Too-hool-hool-zote.

Colonel Miles stationed many soldiers around the camp. No one was allowed in or out. Joseph knew that the colonel hoped to starve his people into surrender.

9

"I Will Fight No More Forever"

For Joseph, the night that followed was the blackest of his life. His dear brother Ollokot was dead. He did not know what would happen to his people —those who had escaped and those who remained.

During that night the women dug trenches with frying pans and camas sticks. Dried meat was fed to the children. Grownups went hungry.

There were no fires. The wind was thick with snow. Children cried. Old people suffered in silence. It was a fearful night.

When morning came, the battle was resumed. The Indians fought from the gullies and trenches.

"Save your ammunition," Joseph told the men. "Fire at the voice that gives a command." Many officers were killed in the battle.

That afternoon Colonel Miles raised a white flag. He asked to talk to Joseph.

"Do not go," Looking Glass urged. "Whites cannot be trusted."

But Joseph went to meet the colonel. "If your people surrender all guns,"

Colonel Miles said, "we will stop the war."

"Let us keep half our rifles," Joseph requested. "We need them to shoot game."

The colonel refused. Joseph started back down the hill, but soldiers grabbed him. Looking Glass was right, Joseph thought. This was the second truce white soldiers had broken. Joseph was rolled in a blanket and put in a tent with mules.

Next morning Yellow Bull came to Colonel Miles' camp with a white flag.

"One of your officers is our prisoner," he said. "Release Chief Joseph or we will kill him."

Colonel Miles released Joseph, and the battle went on.

On the third day Joseph saw many dark objects moving through the snow.

"Sitting Bull!" he exclaimed. "He has come to our rescue!"

His people laughed and shouted in wild relief. Then, as the figures came closer, joy turned to despair. It was only a herd of buffalo!

On the fifth day army scouts again approached the Indian camp with a flag of truce. They brought new surrender terms. The people would be given food and blankets. In the spring they would be sent to the reservation.

Joseph's heart ached for his people. They had lost everything they owned— land, horses, cattle, money. In eleven weeks they had traveled 1,700 miles. They had fought twelve battles without

surrendering. But this time, no victory was possible.

"I am going to surrender," Joseph said to his warriors. "It is for the starving, freezing families. For myself I do not care."

White Bird and Looking Glass would not surrender. They planned to escape to Canada. White Bird and some of his band got away, but Looking Glass was killed by a sniper's bullet.

At four o'clock on the raw, windy afternoon of October 4, 1877, Chief Joseph rode up the hill. Hush-hush-cute and five other warriors went with him. Colonel Miles waited at the half-way mark. General Howard, who had just arrived, was with him.

Joseph swung off his horse. He

handed his rifle to an officer and began to speak:

"Tell General Howard I know his heart . . . I am tired of fighting. Our chiefs are killed . . . Looking Glass is dead. He who led the young men is dead. It is cold and we have no blankets. The little children are freezing to death . . . Hear me, my chiefs. I am tired. My heart is sick and sad. From where the sun now stands, I will fight no more forever."

Then the remaining Nez Perces came up the hill. They gave up their rifles, their horses, and saddles. More than 400 Nez Perces surrendered, including 147 children.

The United States Government did not keep Colonel Miles' promises to Joseph. The Indians were sent to Bismarck, North Dakota; to Leavenworth, Kansas; and finally to Indian Territory. Many died.

Eight long years passed before the destitute Nez Perces were returned to the Northwest. Only 269 remained. Idaho settlers refused to accept Joseph, so his people were sent to Colville Reservation in Washington State. There Joseph died, on September 21, 1904.

Gradually Americans realized that Chief Joseph was a great man, a great leader, and a great humanitarian. Many tributes were paid to his memory. A fine monument was erected and towns, streets, schools, and a ship were named for him. Finally, in June, 1956, Chief Joseph Dam on the Columbia River was dedicated.

Probably Chief Joseph would have preferred another kind of tribute. He would have liked Americans to stop mistreating people of his or any other race. As he said:

"If the white man wants to live in peace with the Indian . . . there need be no trouble. Treat all men alike. Give them all the same laws. Give them all an even chance to live and grow. All men were made by the same Great Spirit. They are brothers."